I Do!

Inspiring thoughts for new brides

Jenny Clements

I Do!

Inspiring thoughts for new brides

Jenny Clements

**Andrews McMeel
Publishing, LLC**

Kansas City

What greater thing is there
for two human souls than to
feel that they are joined . . .

George Eliot

So, you're about to get

married.

It's OK to feel overwhelmed—millions
of lovers have felt overwhelmed before you.

The first step is to

treasure

the reason for your day:

Love.

If love is

spontaneous,

the day can be too.

It's OK to have conflicting

desires.

After all, this is the day that you
can have your cake and eat it.

Just remember to leave some room for change.

Your wedding not only

celebrates

your love for each other,
it also honors your parents and families.

Take pride in your guests.

They are a reflection of who you are.

On the day you
will be a

princess

whose fairy tale
has come true.

Delight in the

opportunity

to show your love
for each other.

And always

remember

to keep expressing it.

It's OK to cry—
most brides do.

Some grooms do too.

Love lets you fly . . .

tradition

grounds you.
Both are priceless.

When it's difficult to find a

balance

between the desires of both families,
bear in mind that they are just
proud and excited.

When you feel like everything is about to
fall apart, remember it's the simple things
that truly matter . . .

your partner, your friends, your family.

Love is about living

in the moment

and creating memories together.

Your wedding day is about sharing your love with the people who are important to you.

Laugh with
all your

heart;

celebrate with all
your soul.

Most importantly,

let go

and be carried away
by the moment.

This book is dedicated to my mom and dad. Through their constant example of love and support for their family, friends, and each other, they have taught me how the power of love allows great things to happen and leads to a life of real fulfilment.

After forty-five years of marriage, mom and dad are still each other's best friend. They have my respect and admiration. I love them dearly.

Michael and Barbara Clements
Married December 4, 1960, London

Special thanks to Julian, Uri, Simon, and the PQ team.
I couldn't have done it without you.

This edition published in 2006 by Andrews McMeel Publishing, LLC, an Andrews McMeel
Universal company, 4520 Main Street, Kansas City, Missouri 64111. No part of this book
may be used or reproduced in any manner whatsoever without written permission except in
the case of reprints in the context of reviews.

The copyrights of the images in this book belong to the following:
Bride Hugging Mother © Royalty-Free/CORBIS; all others are copyright © Getty Images.

Designed by Cameron Gibb

Printed by Midas Printing International Limited, China

ISBN-13: 978-0-7407-5814-0
ISBN-10: 0-7407-5814-4

www.andrewsmcmeel.com